Awaken the

Dreamer

30 Day Inspirational Devotional for Women

**KISHMA A. GEORGE, QUONDA J. WARNER,
SANDRA JACKSON, SHAWNETTE BRAXTON,
RENEE LAWS and PRISTINA MELTON**

Contents

Day 1

H ave you ever asked yourself why were you put on this earth? There was a time when I asked this same question. I could not understand why I was here. I pondered so hard saying, "Why? What is it, Lord? Why am I here?" These questions came at a time in my life when I was going through some difficult moments, which made me seek out my purpose.

Seek out your purpose today! It's okay to ask questions. The word of God says in Matthew 7:7, "Ask and it shall be given; Seek and you will find; Knock and the door will be opened unto you."

MEDITATION SCRIPTURE: Jeremiah 29:11–13~ "For I know the plans I have for you, declares the Lord, plans to prosper you and not to harm you, plans to give you hope and a future. Then you will call on me and come and pray to me, and I will listen to you. You will seek me and find me when you seek me with all your heart."

Day 2

Have you ever thought about what brings you joy? A lot of what we are called to do can be found in our day-to-day activities. For instance, if you find yourself always doing the same thing, that's probably your calling. You may not look at it that way, but if you just pay attention to yourself, to what you do each day, you will see it! Let me give you a clearer example; if you are always giving people advice you may be called to counsel or be a therapist. Whatever holds your interest go for it!

TODAY: Pay close attention to what holds your interest today and your reaction to that interest. How does it make you feel? Are you excited?

MEDITATION SCRIPTURE: Philippians 4:8~ "Finally my brethren, whatsoever things are honest, whatsoever things are just, whatsoever things are pure, whatsoever things are lovely, whatsoever things are of good report; if there be any virtue, and if there be any praise, think on these things."

Day 3

When I was younger, I remember being in my room sitting on my bed, dreaming of the many different businesses that I wanted to open up when I got older. I smiled as I wrote them down! This gave me soo much joy! It felt real, like it was going to happen one day. I was in my happy place when I dreamed of my future!

PROVERBS 16:3: "Commit to the Lord whatever you do, and He will establish your plans."

Today, write down all that you would like to accomplish in your life. Take your time and be specific!

_____

_____

_____

_____

_____

_____

Day 4

Now that you have written down your plans and committed them to the Lord, it is important to pray and ask God for direction. One of my favorite scriptures is Proverbs 3:5–6, which reads, "Trust in the Lord with all your heart; and lean not unto your own understanding, but in all your ways acknowledge him and he will direct your path." Be led by the Lord. For example, if your dream is to become a pediatric nurse and you want to start school, pray to the Lord and see when He wants you to go. You may want to go to school right away, but now may not be the right time. You want to make perfect moves, let God be your guide.

_____

_____

_____

_____

_____

_____

_____

_____

_____

_____

_____

_____

_____

_____

_____

_____

_____

_____

_____

_____

_____

_____

_____

_____

_____

_____

_____

_____

_____

LET US PRAY: Dear Heavenly Father, you are a wonderful, awesome God! I thank you for this individual and how you are grooming them in this moment into what they will become on this earth. Your ways are better than ours and your thoughts are greater. Allow this person to see all of the hinderances that may be in the way of them letting you direct their path. Let them make a sound decision this day in Jesus' name, Amen.

Day 5

There is nothing wrong with doing some research on what you are called to do. You may have even gotten a prophetic word on it. Search it out to get understanding. Get the whys and hows of a thing so you can become who you are called to be. According to the Oxford Dictionary, research is the study of materials and sources in order to establish facts and reach new conclusions. Let's me talk about myself for a sec. I have a cleaning company, and I'm constantly learning daily concerning my business. I even worked for another cleaning company for five months just to understand how a company is run. I did not just go out on my own to that company, I was led of the Lord to go and glean. You see when you are called to a thing and you seek the Lord, He will tell you little by little what to do and how to do it.

Read today Proverbs 25:2 "It is the glory of God to conceal a matter; to search out a matter is the glory of kings." Write down your thoughts concerning this scripture.

Day 6

Isaiah 41:10 says, "Fear not, for I (am) with you; be not dismayed, for I (am) your God: I will strengthen you, I will help you, I will uphold you with my righteous right hand." Wow! How great it is to have someone to be by your side every step of the way. Whether it be a storm, good day, bad day etc., just to know God is with you and for you should give you hope in your dreams today! Follow your dreams and do not look back or fear what's to come or how it will play out. Go on and keep moving forward this day. God has given you the dream(s); trust and believe that He will see it through. Why do we fear? Hmmm... Is it because we don't have the control and since we do not have control we think something may go wrong? See, the dream(s) is really God's purpose for you. He puts it in you so it becomes yours. That's why you have to come into/tap in. It is God Almighty who formed you in the womb with a plan and a purpose and once you understand that, fear is not an option because it is all God. He is our strength and righteousness.

LET US PRAY: Heavenly Father, you are awesome in all of your ways. You created us in your image and likeness and have given each of us a purpose and a plan to fulfill in this life. You have even blessed us with angels to help with our assignments. We will not speak death but life over everything you have prepared for us and anything that we may have spoken death on bring to our remembrance so that we will make it right before you in Jesus' name, Amen!

TODAY'S TASK: Write down a declaration for your dreams and recite it daily!

_____

_____

_____

_____

_____

_____

_____

_____

_____

_____

_____

_____

_____

_____

_____

_____

_____

_____

_____

_____

_____

_____

_____

_____

_____

_____

_____

_____

_____

_____

_____

_____

_____

_____

_____

_____

Day 7

L et today be your center of interest. Focus, focus, focus on those dreams. How are they coming along? Are you distracted? The dreams God has given you are His ways. So why not give your undivided attention to them? Take at least 20–30 minutes a day to commit to your dreams and see how God will add daily unto you. He will give you more and more pieces to work on each day and before you know it you will be pouring out, overflowing in your purpose. People will began to see your dream for what it is and you will not have to convince them. Your dream will be your reality!

_____

_____

_____

_____

_____

_____

_____

Encouragement: Psalm 119:15 encourages us to meditate on God's precepts and fix our eyes on His ways! You can do it—stay focused! Put on some music and go for it! Let nothing stop you today!

Day 8

"Awaken the dreamer in you" means not to sleep on yourself; not to sleep on what God has blessed you with. You ever fell asleep while someone was talking to you? Lol, I'm pretty sure you would not want that to happen to you. Stay awake, you have a legacy to fulfill that will go on for generations. Pass down those dreams to your family. I thank God that dreams were passed down to me through my family line. What will you leave if you sleep on your hopes of becoming who God wants you to be? Some will die not ever able to fulfill what God has given them. Unemptied, unhappy, frustrated, and sorrowful. God gives chance after chance. Don't let it be you who gets left behind. There are dreams dreamed by some of your family members who have passed away and those dreams were never accomplished. So will you continue to follow your dreams?

Lord, I pray that the person who has read through these pages will not only fulfill their dreams but the dreams of others that were left behind. My God, thank you for this opportunity for them to pick up the pieces and move forward in you without any fear, knowing that you are here and are able to complete the work in them. I pray that they will come to know the depth and height of your love and a deeper relationship with you that will forever change their lives. I thank you for drawing them, my Lord, and it is in your name and all for your glory in Jesus' name, Amen.

Day 9

The Lord is birthing you out! Can you tell? Here's the thing; when you feel like running, when you feel like you no longer can take the pain, when you've had enough, when giving up seems like your only option, it's time to birth out. A woman giving birth physically cannot run from it, she has to endure; she has to get that baby out! If you're feeling frustrated today, it could be that you are in labor and ready to deliver! Remember producing is never comfortable and if you are comfortable you are not growing or birthing anything! Get in a quiet place and take a minute to relax because your birthing is at hand!

SCRIPTURE MEDITATION: Psalm 46:5

"God is in the midst of her, she shall not be moved; God shall help her, just at the break of dawn." NKJV

Day 10

God has equipped you for your next level. He has released you to go forth. Thus, says the Lord, arise and go forth in my boldness for it is here. You've been through the downs and tested with the things that I have given you. Now you are able to stand when the things of old and new come your way! I am proud of you, daughter! Again, I say your next level is here, arise for I have "awakened the dreamer" in you!

Isn't it so amazing how God works? He does things when we are not even thinking about them. He gives us everything we need to complete every assignment He has bestowed upon us. We can accomplish anything because of Him alone. As you continue reading this devotional, **MY PRAYER FOR YOU** is that you receive all that God has for you and a greater thirst for Him to be released over you in Jesus' name, Amen!

MEDITATION READINGS: 2 Peter 1:3; 2 Thessalonians 1:2–11

Day 11

Forgive Yourself

Free yourself—take accountability where you went wrong and forgive yourself wholeheartedly. You may need to forgive yourself and that is why we need God; He gives us strength to forgive ourselves. You do not have to carry all that luggage and fight those battles. Your battles belong to God; release them all period, now, so that you have forgiven yourself and can flow and do what God has called you to do, more productively, and now you are free.

SCRIPTURE OF THE DAY: Psalms 32:5

"I acknowledge my sin unto thee, and mine iniquity have I not had. I said, I will confess my transgressions unto the Lord and now forgavest the iniquity of mine. Selah"

MY PRAYER FOR YOU: Lord, I thank you for waking me up

today in my right mind. Lord, I ask you to give me strength today to forgive myself where I have come short. I thank you and I praise you and I glorify your Holy name. I know unforgiveness to oneself is a form of self-sabotage. I will no longer hold unforgiveness in my heart. God, help me and strengthen me to do so; I give you all the glory, the honor and the praise, Amen.

Day 12

The Truth about You

If you want to know the truth, then look in the mirror; your reflection is not just what you see, it's also what you do. The mirror gives us a reflection of the outside. A self-check is a reflection from within. When doing a self-check, you must be honest with yourself; this is vital for your growth. If you are determined to be the best you then be honest with yourself, you owe you that much. A self-check has great benefits that can help you be your authentic self, to discover more to you than you see with your natural eyes. Remember the mirror will reveal your beauty as well.

SCRIPTURE OF THE DAY: 2 Corinthians 13:5

"Examine yourselves, whether ye be in the faith; prove your own selves. Know ye not your own selves, how that Jesus Christ is in you, except ye be reprobates?" (KJV)

Test yourselves to see if you are in the faith; examine

yourselves! Or do you not recognize this about yourselves, that Jesus Christ is in you-- unless indeed you fail the test? (NASB)

Day 13

You Are ....

You are a Winner! God, you are blessed to see another day. You are beautiful and powerful. Apply God's Word to every situation that may look bigger than your faith; God's Word is our weapon, you are a Winner, and Victory is your name. You mean so much to so many people, you are an important piece to so many others' puzzles. Your love, kindness, and compassion display who God is. You are the light to someone's darkness, an answered prayer to someone's issue. God chose you and gave you strength to get through today one step at a time, you are not alone! Have an amazing day because you are amazing.

SCRIPTURE OF THE DAY: Genesis 1:27

"So God created mankind in his own image, in the image of God he created them; male and female he created them."

REPEAT THIS PRAYER: God, I thank you for waking me up in my right mind. God, I ask you to continue to display the fruits of the spirit: love, joy, peace, long suffering, gentleness, faith, meekness, and temperance within me. I thank you for your love and guidance that you continue to show daily.

Day 14

You Are God's Creation

Hello, Beautiful, you are more than a conqueror; you are the head and not the tail. No, matter what you face today, you are still a Winner, you are simply amazing. You are courageous and bold. You must continue being who God made you to be. Go for it, if God gave you an opportunity take a leap, you will not fall, God's hands are big enough to catch you. Go spread your awesomeness to the world and shine like the star you are.

SCRIPTURE OF THE DAY: Matthew 5:16

"Let your light shine before men, that they may know your good works, and glorify your Father who is in heaven."

REPEAT THIS PRAYER: God, I thank you for giving me the mind of Christ. I ask you, God, to continue to allow your light to shine within me. I thank you for making me in your image, so

I can do greater works. I thank you for making me courageous and bold to fulfill your purpose that is in me. Allow me to have the discernment to know when to take a leap of faith. I know that you will never forsake me. I appreciate that you open doors of opportunity.

Day 15

Only You Can Do It!

Hello, Beautiful, you are unique, and irreplaceable. Only you can do what God told you to do. God has given you specific instructions to walk and live out your purpose. You got this, Sis, keep your head up and continue to look to the hills from which cometh your help. Yes, at times people will not understand what God has told you to do. Do It anyway, no matter what you feel Do It anyways. God gave it to you, so just DO IT. You have all the ingredients that God needs for you to accomplish the mission.

SCRIPTURE OF THE DAY: Isaiah 41:10

"Fear thou not; for I am thy God: I will strengthen thee: be not dismayed; for I am thy God: I will strengthen thee; yea, I will help thee; yea, I will up hold thee with the right hand of my righteousness."

REPEAT THIS PRAYER: God, I thank you for giving me the mind of Christ. I thank you for creating me to be unique and giving me the strength to embrace my uniqueness. When you speak, I will listen, even if I do not understand, because I trust you. I know you will not steer me wrong. I thank you for all the love and patience that you give me; I need you like never before to complete what you have entrusted me to do, to bring glory to your name. Thank you and Amen.

Day 16

I Celebrate You

Hello, Beautiful, look at what you have accomplished, you have come so far, look at you now, you go, Sis, I celebrate you. You work so hard to complete your goals and work towards your destiny; I like how you are so organized and balanced. I love the way you carry yourself, you are such a Queen. Oh my, you are such a giver to your community and the people around you. You have such patience and compassion for everyone; you treat everyone with respect and God's love. God must be smiling at you because you resemble Him so much. I am so glad that you are my Sister.

SCRIPTURE FOR THE DAY: Ephesians 5:8

"For at one time you were darkness, but now you are light in the Lord. Walk as children of light."

PRAYER FOR THE DAY: God, I thank you for giving me the mind of Christ, continue to help me grow in you. I thank you for displaying order in my life; I thank you for giving balance; I thank you for the push you give me on a daily basis to bring me closer to you and my destiny. God, I thank you for allowing me to experience your love and faithfulness. Thank you and Amen.

Day 17

You Have the Most Committed Investor

Hello, Beautiful, you are so blessed; you have God, the most faithful and committed Investor that you have on your team. God is always on time and He has no excuses, remember to always rely on God as you walk in your destiny. God downloads wisdom, understanding and strategies in our spirits. If we listen and look, we can see Him speaking, He always wants to talk with us. God wants the best for you and what He placed in you it shall not come back void. God's timing is the best timing. Know that you have unlimited support through God; if He gave you the vision, He will give you the provision.

SCRIPTURE OF THE DAY: James 3:17

"But the wisdom that is from above is first pure, then peaceable, gentle, easy to be intreated, full of mercy and good fruits, without partiality, and without hypocrisy."

God, thank you for giving me a mind of Christ, I thank you for your wisdom and guidance that you give me daily. I thank you for covering and protecting every idea that you download in me. I thank you for understanding me and loving me. I love you, God. Thank you and Amen.

Day 18

The Jewels within You Let Them Shine

G ood morning Beautiful, be encouraged; the jewel God put within you need to shine. You have purpose within you that others need to see, you are one of a kind. When God made you, He had a reason. Dream BIG and be consistent working towards your goals. Your persistence always overcomes resistance, always remember this. Keep pushing forward, you must see your dreams through. Your dreams shall come to a reality. Today is the day that God hath made; you shall rejoice and be glad in it. Rejoice, you are chosen!

SCRIPTURE FOR THE DAY: Jeremiah 17: 7

"But blessed is the one who trusts in the Lord, whose confidence is in him."

REPEAT THIS PRAYER: I thank you for waking me up in my

right mind today, God. I ask for you to help me be more confident in you and not myself. Help me remember to always seek the Kingdom of God first; this gives me more confidence. Help me see your purpose in my life so I can continue to allow your light to shine through me.

Day 19

Know Your Season

G ood morning Beautiful, you matter. I know there is so much to do, know that there is a season for everything. Please do not be anxious for anything, be patient in all that you do and give it to God. Know what season you are in. You do not want to be out of season, you do not want to move too fast or move too slowly, seek God to know what He is saying. Pray daily and listen daily, so many times we are in a rush to do what we think is right. God has given us a manual and that is the Bible and He has given us the Holy Spirit to lead us. Be sensitive to how the Holy Spirit is leading and, yes, a lot of times how we are led doesn't make sense, lean not to your own understanding.

SCRIPTURE OF THE DAY: Proverbs 3:5–6

"Trust in the Lord with all thine heart; and lean not unto thine own understanding. In all thy ways acknowledge him, and he shall direct your paths."

REPEAT PRAYER: God, I thank you for waking me up in my right mind. God, I ask that you download patience and confidence to do the things that you would have me to do. I want to please you in all my ways. Give me the discernment to know what season I am in so the fruit with me can be healthy. God, I want to do your will for my life, I surrender my own agenda to pick up your agenda wholeheartedly. Thank you.

Day 20

It's Your Time!

Hello, Beautiful, step out in faith. See yourself where you want to be; if you can see it you can achieve it. Pray and be a doer of the Word of God. God has promised us so much, if we just take Him at his Word there are no limits. They lied when they told you the sky is the limit; we are limitless through Jesus Christ. The Bible says we can do all things through Jesus Christ who strengthens us. All is a word that means the whole quantity. There is nothing you cannot do, it is how BIG your FAITH is. I challenge you to exercise your faith more.

SCRIPTURE OF THE DAY: Mark 11:24 KJV

"Therefore I say unto you, What things soever ye desire, when ye pray, believe that ye receive them, and ye shall have them."

REPEAT PRAYER: God, I thank you for giving me the mind of

Christ. God, I thank you for downloading within me my heart's desires. I thank you for opening my eyes to see that I need to enlarge my faith and belief in you and your Word. Only your Word will give me more confidence in using my faith. Faith without works is dead. I choose today to exercise my faith more. Thank you and Amen.

Day 21

Awaken My Child

A waken, my child, from your dream. It's time to arise and start your day. While you were sleeping I was planning out your day for everything you will need each step of the way. Concentrate on me, keep your eyes and ears open. Let my Holy Spirit lead and guide you. He will protect you from danger seen and unseen. Trust yourself in His care for I know the plans I have for you. Remember, follow me one step at a time. Don't go ahead of me. Trust me when you can't see me or just don't understand. I need you to pause; breathe you out and me in and call upon my name and you will feel me near.

COMMIT TO HEART: "But when the truth-giving Spirit comes, he will unveil the reality of every truth within you. He won't speak his own message, but only what he hears from the Father, and he will reveal prophetically to you what is to come." John 16:13 (TPT)

"For I know the plans and thoughts that I have for you,' says the Lord, 'plans for peace and well-being and not for disaster, to give you a future and a hope." Jeremiah 29:11 (AMP)

LET'S PRAY TOGETHER: Father God, thank you for waking me up this morning. I am ready to fulfill the plans you have for my life. Thank you for giving me the strength and the power I need to stay focused. Thank you for your Holy Spirit that provides protection and guidance as He leads me through the day. I will trust you and call upon your name for I know you will never leave or forsake me in Jesus' name, Amen.

Day 22

The Journey Begins

As your journey begins it's going to take perseverance. It's going to take you seeking my face not just my hand in order to stay on the right path. On this journey you will face some challenges and difficulties along the way, but I need you to stay focused. I will teach you how to maximize every opportunity in the face of opposition. You must trust me and know it will work out for your good. Do not give into fear or worry; they will only rob you of your peace and joy. Instead of trying to anticipate problems before they come, trust me enough to face them as they come.

COMMIT TO HEART: "You will keep in [a]perfect and constant peace the one whose mind is steadfast [that is, committed and focused on You—in both [b]inclination and character],Because he trusts and takes refuge in You [with hope and confident expectation]." Isiah 26:3 AMP

Though we experience every kind of pressure, we're not crushed. At times we don't know what to do, but quitting is not an option. We are persecuted by others, but God has not forsaken us. We may be knocked down, but not out. 2 Corinthians 4:8-9 (TPT)

LET US PRAY TOGETHER: Father God, thank you for helping me on this journey. I know with you on my side I will persevere when obstacles come my way. I will stay focused, slow down and tightly Hold Your Hand even when I face opposition. I will not fear or become weary; instead I will trust you that, no matter what, it will work out for my good in Jesus' name, Amen.

Day 23

Moving Forward

It's time to move forward and walk boldly on the path I have dreamed for you. Trust in me, your Lord, with all your heart and do not depend on your own understanding. Seek my will in all you do and I will show you which path to take. I am a shelter and strength, always ready to help in times of trouble. Walk in confidence as you fix your eyes on me. Whenever you feel uneasy remember that I am holding you up with my right hand. There is nothing that can separate you from me. Rest in me knowing that nothing is too hard or impossible for your God. Focus on me and give me your full attention as we move forward in purpose together.

COMMIT TO HEART: "Remember that I have commanded you to be determined and confident! Do not be afraid or discouraged, for I, the LORD your God, am with you wherever you go." Joshua 1:9 (GNT)

'The LORD is my strength and my [impenetrable] shield; My heart trusts [with unwavering confidence] in Him, and I am helped; Therefore, my heart greatly rejoices, and with my song I shall thank Him and praise Him." Psalms 28:7 (AMP)

LET US PRAY TOGETHER: Father God, thank you for moving me forward so that I am no longer stagnated. You have designed me to walk with confidence and boldness on this journey with you. My eyes are fixed on you. Regardless of what someone says or tries to do I know you have my back. No one can stop me from fulfilling my God-given dream in Jesus' name, Amen.

Day 24

Created on Purpose to Fulfill a Purpose

M y Love, you were not a mistake. You were created on purpose for a purpose. You ask the question why are you are here? The answer is very simple. To fulfill purpose. I planned the day you would be born and how it will take you to fulfil my purpose for you. Know this; my plan and purpose for you took into account every error and sin. I don't make mistakes. I created you to love. You were custom designed in my mind. It's now time to view purpose from My eyes. I want to show you things you've never seen, heard of or ever imagined. Open your heart and allow Me to come in. My desire to use you to fulfill the plan I have for your life. It's time to dream. Let Me share My deepest thoughts and secrets with you. Let Me take you on a journey and show you amazing and wonderful things that I have planned for you.

COMMIT TO HEART: "So, we are convinced that every detail of our lives is continually woven together to fit into God's perfect plan of bringing good into our lives, for we are his lovers who have been called to fulfill his designed purpose." Romans 8:28 (TPT) "God is not like people, who lie; He is not a human who changes his mind. Whatever, He promises, he does; He speaks, and it is done." Number 23:19 (GNT)

LET US PRAY TOGETHER: Father God, thank you that my life has purpose. Thank you for loving me. I know I was designed for purpose. Use me for your glory. Thank you that seeds of greatness are in me. Thank you for seeing me as valuable, capable and trustworthy. Thank you for using my life to fulfill purpose and make your dreams come true in Jesus' name, Amen.

Day 25

The Power to Forgive

Forgiveness is a gift that you give yourself. Sometimes, holding on to unforgiveness can make you bitter and angry. That is not my best for you. Don't infect your future. Trust me to heal your hurt. Trust me to help you though the loss. I know you may not think you can forgive because someone hurt you so badly. Someone you loved deeply betrayed you, let me deal with that person. My child, when you forgive it takes away their power to hurt you anymore. The longer you hold on to unforgiveness the more it disconnects you from me. I want the best for your life. Forgive them so I can forgive you.

COMMIT TO HEART: "Later Peter approached Jesus and said, "How many times do I have to forgive my fellow believer who keeps offending me? Seven times? Jesus answered, "Not seven times, Peter, but seventy times seven times" Matthew 18:21-22 (TPT)

"We are destroying sophisticated arguments and every exalted and proud thing that sets itself up against the [true] knowledge of God, and we are taking every thought and purpose captive to the obedience of Christ." 2 Corinthians10:5 (AMP)

LET US PRAY TOGETHER: Father God, thank you for the power to forgive that sets me free. I ask forgiveness for the negative and harmful words I have spoken. Transform my thoughts. Lord, I forgive my offender. Help me to heal inside and out. Help me to release the hurt and begin to love like you. I no longer want to poison my future. Change my words that they are pleasing in your sight. Please forgive me and restore my relationship with you.

Day 26

God's Perfect Timing

My perfect timing is giving birth to what I have put in you. Believe that conception has taken place. Believe you are pregnant with my promises. I know you have been waiting a long time. Embracing the process is crucial. While in the process you are being taught, trained, matured, pruned and prepared. Learning to trust Me is a fulfilling purpose. Stop telling yourself it's never going to happen. My timing is not your timing. I have everything under control. Don't hesitate when I give you instructions. My protection, provision and favor are all connected to my timing and your obedience. Dream it, believe it, and in my perfect timing you will achieve it.

COMMIT TO HEART: "Within your heart you can make plans for your future, but the Lord chooses the steps you take to get there." Proverbs 16:9 (TPT)

"For the vision is yet for the appointed [future] time It hurries toward the goal [of fulfillment]; it will not fail. Even though it delays, wait [patiently] for it, Because it will certainly come; it will not delay." Habakkuk 2:3 (AMP)

LET US PRAY TOGETHER: Father God, thank you for your perfect timing. Thank you for being an on-time God. Give me a clear vision of what you need me to do. I do believe, but help my unbelief. As I wait on your perfect timing help me to walk by faith and not by sight until my dreams come to pass in Jesus' name, Amen.

Day 27

I Am a Promise Keeper

I am a promise maker and a promise keeper; I need you to hold on to these four words. I AM WITH YOU. The first two words are my signature that validates my promises to you. I am Abba Father; I am your Miracle Worker. I am your Way-Maker. I am your Deliverer. I am your Vindicator. I am your Healer and your Provider. The last two words are used to seal who I made the promise to and that is WITH YOU.

The Bible contains every written agreement that I have promised you. When you read the Bible, my voice will be heard through every spoken word. You will see and hear what I am saying and know that I am who I say I am. This Covenant is for a lifetime. It is a guarantee of my love, faithfulness and commitment to you. There are two immutable things you must know about me. The first thing is that it is impossible for me, God, to lie. Once I have spoken my promise I cannot change my mind. The second thing is I sealed my promise with an oath that cannot be broken. My child, it's time to walk out your God-given dream.

COMMIT TO HEART: "The steps of a [good and righteous] man are directed and established by the LORD, And He delights in his way [and blesses his path]. When he falls, he will not be hurled down,

Because the LORD is the One who holds his hand and sustains him." Psalms 37:23-24 (AMP)

Therefore know [without any doubt] and understand that the LORD your God, He is God, the faithful God, who is keeping His covenant and His [steadfast] lovingkindness to a thousand generations with those who love Him and keep His commandments; Deuteronomy 7:9 (AMP)

LET US PRAY TOGETHER: Father God, thank you for being a promise maker and keeper. Thank you for your faithfulness to your Word. I promise to honor my vows; to love you with all my heart and with all my soul and with all my mind and all my strength and Love my neighbor as myself in Jesus' name, Amen.

Day 28

Walk It Out

My child, it's time to rise up and walk. Shift from your posture and stand. Shift your position and walk. Shift your mind and pursue and conquer. Change your strategy; speak life over dreams. Your words have power. What you say does matter, it does make a difference. It's time to walk it out. Shift—forgive the unforgivable, shift—you are the head and not the tail, shift—you are above and not beneath, shift—you are a lender and not a borrower, shift and pursue your dreams, shift and conquer your fears. I have not given you a spirit of fear but of love, power and a sound mind. Shift—pray what you want not what you don't want. Declare and decree and I will establish it. Rise up, don't settle for being ordinary; I have made you extraordinary. Rise up and walk in victory.

COMMIT TO HEART: "Yet even in the midst of all these things, we triumph over them all, for God has made us to be more than conquerors, and his demonstrated love is our glorious victory over everything!" Romans 8:37 (TPT)

"But whether I live or die is not important, for I don't esteem my life as indispensable.[a] It's more important for me to fulfill my destiny and to finish the ministry my Lord Jesus has assigned to me, which is to faithfully preach the wonderful news of God's grace." Acts 20:24 (TPT)

LET US PRAY TOGETHER: Father God, thank you for this day to rise up and walk it out. Thank you for the shift. I declare and decree I will not let anyone stand in my way of pursuing my dreams. Nor will I allow anything that would try to separate me and you from walking hand in hand in Jesus' name, Amen.

Day 29

Hand in Hand

I knew you before you were born. Every day of your life is recorded in my book. I laid out every moment before a single day had passed. Your story ends in Victory. I have taken into account every aspect of your life. I know every loss you will encounter, every disappointment that will happen and has happened including every challenge and setback. Hear me, my child, your story ends in Victory. I see the desires of your heart and they line up with my Word and my will and my plan for your life. As your Father in Heaven let me say this to you; the final chapter of your life ends with you fulfilling your God-given purpose. Let go of the past. Hold on to my unchanging hand. Let us walk through this journey of life together one moment, one day at a time, hand in hand. So, dream and dream again knowing I will be with you every step of the way.

COMMIT TO HEART: "But when God, who had chosen me and set me apart before I was born, and called me through His grace, was pleased to reveal His Son in me so that I might preach Him among the Gentiles [as the good news—the way of salvation], I did not immediately consult with anyone [for guidance regarding God's call and His revelation to me]." Galatians 1:15-16 (AMP)

"but thanks be to God, who gives us the victory [as conquerors] through our Lord Jesus Christ. Therefore, my beloved brothers and sisters, be steadfast, immovable, always excelling in the work of the Lord [always doing your best and doing more than is needed], being continually aware that your labor [even to the point of exhaustion] in the Lord is not futile nor wasted [it is never without purpose]." 1 Corinthians 15:57-58 (AMP)

LET US PRAY TOGETHER: Father God, thank you for the victory. I feel safe in the palm of your hand; I will walk in the freedom that you gave me, I choose to stop living in the past. I choose to stop rehearsing past disappointments and failures. I choose to stop focusing on past rejection. I choose to walk hand in hand with you. For my latter shall be greater than my past. It's time for me to let go so I can dream again.

Day 30

It's Time to Dream Again

My dearest love, you are free to be you. I have fearfully and wonderfully made you. Do not compare yourself to anyone else, it is a distraction. It will rob you of your hopes, dreams and energy. You are my masterpiece. Dream again, my child. I created you with a purpose for a purpose. Dream again, you are empowered and equipped to do everything I have called you to do. Stay away from the spirit of competition. The race is not given to the Swift. Run your own race. Use your gifts, all your talents and skills, for my glory. This will allow you to see my blessings and favor in your life. Dream again, you are my messenger. Trust that I am with you even if you make a mistake or it doesn't turn out the way you planned. Don't stop dreaming—dream and dream again, I have dispatched my angels to help you along the way. Don't get weary in well-doing but know that in due season you will reap if you faint not.

COMMIT TO HEART: "but just as it is written [in Scripture], "THINGS WHICH THE EYE HAS NOT SEEN AND THE EAR HAS NOT HEARD, AND WHICH HAVE NOT ENTERED THE HEART OF MAN, ALL THAT GOD HAS PREPARED FOR THOSE WHO LOVE HIM [who hold Him in affectionate reverence, who obey Him, and who gratefully recognize the benefits that He has bestowed]." 1 Cor 2:9 (AMP)

"This is what I will do in the last days I will pour out my Spirit on everybody and cause your sons and daughters to prophesy, and your young men will see visions, and your old men will experience dreams from God." Acts 2:17 (GNT)

LET US PRAY TOGETHER: Father God, thank you that I am free to dream again and again. I am free from comparing myself to others. I am so thankful that my steps are ordered by you. Even though I'm not perfect I thank you, God, for doing a perfect work in me in Jesus' name, Amen.

Dream Affirmations

FULLY CONVINCED

So we are convinced that every detail of our lives is continually woven together to fit into God's perfect plan of bringing good into our lives for we are His lover who has been called to fulfill His designed purpose.

Romans 8:28

Dear Heavenly Father

I thank you for your will and your way. I thank you that no weapon formed against me shall prosper and every tongue that rises up against me shall be condemned, but I am grateful to be convinced during times of despair that He who has begun a good work in me shall perform it until the days of Jesus Christ... Amen. Sometimes, as you walk this thing called life, you will run into some roadblocks, tests and even trials, but you must remain convinced that during this test the Master Jesus Christ has your prayers and dreams all in control.

ENCOURAGE YOURSELF WHEN NO ONE IS AROUND

When life knocks you down, brush yourself off and quickly look up and encourage yourself, the first step is to turn in faith and seek God. There is no substitute for this—Trust God.

Dear God,

I pray that whoever will read this at whatever time, moment or season in their life it will bring them peace, encouragement, and clarity of thinking. God, I thank you that when they are unsure, they can come to you for assurance. God, I speak encouragement to the Dreamer that may be reading this book right now and I say, "Keep Dreaming. God is not like man that He shall lie; neither is He like the son of man that He shall repent." There comes a time in every Dreamer's life when we feel like we are at a standstill. NO, you are just in holding position, waiting to meet the person to calibrate your purpose.

FAITHFUL IS ALL YOU HAVE

"A faithful man will abound with blessings." Abound is defined as to occur or exist in great quantities or numbers; to be rich or well supplied; to be filled. ~Proverbs 28:20

Dear Heavenly Father,

I thank you for being such a faithful God concerning your people. God teaches us how to activate that same characteristic that lies within us. God, I decree and declare that I will remain faithful over the Dreams that you placed within my heart and declare to stand on Habakkuk 2:2 until it comes to pass in Jesus' name, Amen.

BEING CHOSEN IS A GOOD THING

"For many are called but few are chosen."

~ Matthew 22:14

Dear My Chosen One,

I pray for you this morning that you will be encouraged, enlightened, and motivated to keep pressing to your Dreams knowing like Jeremiah 29:11 that He who has begun a good work shall perform it until the day of Jesus Christ. Everything that you have dream or will dream and it aligns up with your purpose has to be fulfilled, just remember in those times when you feel stuck that God is not a man that He shall lie neither the Son of Man that He shall repent. God is a promise keeper, way maker, miracle worker. Keep Dreaming, Keep Writing, it's going to come to pass.

PRAISE IS YOUR WEAPON

"I will exalt you, my God the King, I will praise your name forever and ever. Every day I will praise you and extol your name forever and ever. Great is the Lord and most worthy of praise for His greatness no one can fathom." ~ Psalm 145

Dear Heavenly Father,

I pray for the Dreamers that will come in contact with this book. God allows them to feel a reigning power from Him and gives them a clarifying mind to journal down the next part of the phase of their dream. Help them to stay hand and hand with you as they continue to walk out dreams and purpose with you. I bind the spirit of discouragement and lose the spirit of Hope. Thank you, God, for being a God, for being a hearer of all prayers in Jesus' name, Amen.

DON'T BE NAÏVE, USE WISDOM

"If any of you lack wisdom, let him ask of God, that giveth to all men liberally, and upbraideth not, and it shall be given him."

~ James 1:5

Good Morning Holy Spirit,

I am thankful for this opportunity to be able to boldly approach your throne seeking wisdom concerning guidance for my Dreams. Without you, God, I don't know if this will ever become possible. Help me with your wisdom in everything I do concerning my Dreams from who I collaborate with for my dreams. God, in those times when I get a mental block, help me to turn to you for help. God, I thank you for allowing me to make it to another decade in time, which means I'm embarking on new opportunities for my Dreams. Help me to realize that there is strength in wisdom when you actually listen and apply to your life when it is necessary in Jesus' name, Amen.

WORSHIP WHEN YOU DON'T UNDERSTAND

"God is a Spirit: and they that worship him must worship him in spirit and in truth."

~ John 4:24

Our God our Father teaches me how to find a place of worship when I don't understand. I know that worship is defined as the feeling or expression of reverence and adoration for deity. God teaches us, oh God, that worship is just as important as praise but it must be in spirit and in truth. Help the persons who will read this chapter to know that worship is a secret place that will lead us back to you for comfort and revelation to remain steadfast and unmovable until you bless us. God, for all the dreamers that need help and guidance on where next to go help them find a place of worship in you in Jesus' name, Amen.

BE GRATEFUL FOR EVERYTHING

"Rejoice always, pray continually. Give thanks in all circumstances; for this is God's will for you in Christ Jesus."

~ 1 Thessalonians 5:16–18

One of my favorite songs is "Be Grateful". That song has got me through many dark nights and has taught me to be grateful for things that seem little as blessings because there is always someone worse off than us. Dear God, I pray that whoever comes across this prayer today will not take anything that they are blessed with for granted to help them realize that without you and your tender mercies nothing could be possible including the fulfillment of their dreams and desires. I ask that you help me to apply a mind of gratitude in everything I do concerning my life in Jesus' name, Amen.

STAY HUMBLE IN BECOMING WEALTHY

"But remember the LORD your God, for it is he who gives you the ability to produce wealth, and so confirms his covenant, which he swore to your ancestors, as it is today."

~ Deuteronomy 8:18

Dear Most Gracious Father,

Thank you for allowing us to come and dwell in your presence. Thank you for coming with all our concern. God, I thank you ever so much for being a very present God. I know you promised me that you are a provider and will meet all of our needs according to your riches and glory, help me not to mishandle the wealth of riches you have in store for me; help me to always consult you in all my financial endeavors so that I might stay on the right road with the plan for my life in Jesus' name, Amen.

PRAYER

"Then you will call upon me and come and pray to me, and I will hear you."

~ Jeremiah 29:12

Dear Heavenly Father,

I thank you for leaving us with instructions on how to pray. Thank you for helping us to understand that praying is important, it is like the gas in a car and like the oxygen to a body. God, help us to understand that until we understand the greatness of prayer, we will never understand the greatness within ourselves. Father, prayer helps the Dreamer within us understand that to fully be able to unleash the Dreamer within us we must unleash the pray warrior within you. The prayer warrior and the Dreamer go hand and hand you can't have one without the other. God, help us to develop our prayer language with you so that we will be able to touch you in prayer in Jesus' name, Amen.

Empowerment Affirmations

MAKE ME OVER

Maker *Get to Know Your Maker

Accept *Accept Who You Are

Knowledge *Knowledge Is Power

Enlightened *Shine Bright

Mature *Growth is Necessary

Effective *Production

Optimistic *Staying Positive

Value *Know Your Worth

Everlasting Love *Your Forever

Reborn *I am

Maker "Get to Know Your Maker"

Have you ever just sat and though about who created you and what you were created for? Like what was the purpose of your very existence? I want you to know you're not alone. I can remember attending church as a little girl with my parents, questioning who this man was they called Jesus and who was this God they served. As time went by I went to church with my siblings without my parents, and I began to learn more and more about God, Adam and Eve, and God's son, Jesus. It made me question so many things in my life. The more I was taught the more I realized that God was the maker and He placed purpose in every one of us. It may not be revealed to you all at once, but the more you learn of Him, sooner or later the pieces will come all together in what you truly are purposed for.

I want to pray these words with you: *Dear Heavenly Father, place a desire in my heart to get to know you and to truly fulfill what I am purposed to do in life. You are the maker and I am the clay, mold me into the woman or man you want me to become.*

Reference Scriptures:

Genesis 2:5 From the beginning Adam and Eve had purpose.

Who is God? Isaiah 41:13, Zephaniah 3:17, Hebrews 3:4, 1 John 4:2, 1 John 1:1, 1 John 4:8

Purpose: Romans 8:28, Proverbs 16:4

Ecclesiastes 3:1

ACCEPT "ACCEPT WHO YOU ARE"

I want you to get a mirror, look at yourself very closely. Perhaps even get a full body mirror, and tell yourself, "I love me, I accept me." You may not feel that way, but there's power in what we speak. It doesn't matter what walk of life we come from, God accepts us. He knew you before your every existence. Oftentimes we beat ourselves up, more than giving ourselves a pat on the back. Nobody is perfect, and I pray that from this day forward you will fall in love with yourself and know you are accepted by God. Remember He has fearfully and wonderfully made you.

Psalms 139:14

KNOWLEDGE "KNOWLEDGE IS POWER"

The more you educate yourself the more productive you will become in life. It expands your perspective and helps you become more confident communicating and preforming a task or goal. The Bible says in Hosea 4:6, "My people perish for the lack of knowledge." It is important that we continue to educate ourselves so we won't be lost. Whether it be the news, learning more about God, a particular class, degree , trade, or job training . To know is better than not knowing or being lost.

Hosea 4:6

ENLIGHTENED "SHINE BRIGHT"

One of my favorite songs is "This little light of mine, I'm going to let it shine." I used to look at the stars in the sky at night and ask my dad, "What star is that one? Then I'd count how many stars I could see and say, "I am the brightest star." Right where you are, I want you to visualize yourself as being the brightest star in the sky, so radiant with glow and sparkle. Once you have found Him, accepted yourself, and become knowledgeable of His love and ways, you can shine soooo bright that you will began to beam off others. You were born to shine, a naturalist—Shine Bright.

Matt 5:16, Psalms 119:105

MATURE "GROWTH IS NECESSARY"

There's nothing worse than seeing everyone grow around you and you feel like you're in a dead place. You begin to ask yourself, "Why am I not growing?" It can be a number of things; it's not your season or it's about how you applied the information you learned and are continuing to learn. Some people reach a place and choose not to learn anymore, they set limits. Take the time to sit any think, *Did I place limits on myself? Am I open to excel past the place I am?* There are age restrictions for a reason on various items and places and we as an adult we cannot act like a child at 27. Unfortunately, in society we see it all the time, and most of the time that person remains in the same place every time you see them until something happens and causes them to mature, or some maybe never. Don't let the word *never* stagnant you. Growth is necessary, and I'm praying that you give up *never*, and began to walk into unbelievable opportunities, and excel to the next level.

1 Corinthians 13:11

EFFECTIVE "PRODUCTION"

Just like the grass grows every day and the fruit trees bear fruit, so is it that God wants us to be productive (Gen 1:11). He made Adam and Eve so we may be fruitful and multiply and leave a generation. Unfortunately, not every one of us can naturally produce, but in so many other ways we are producers. It takes more than one, and if we all work together, we will help everyone gets what they need to be effective. Just watch where you're seeds are being produced because some may fall on bad soil, meaning be careful where you give most of your energy to because it may take the time or place of where you could be the most effective .Be wise; time is valuable and God expects us to produce and be prosperous.

Luke 8:8, Zechariah 8:12

OPTIMISTIC "STAYING POSITIVE"

You often hear the phrase, "We are what we speak." That statement isn't always true because people can be very cruel with their words towards themselves or others. Being positive can be a very hard task, especially when adversity is among you. Even though it's one of the hardest tasks being optimistic, staying positive can change the whole situation or your ability to maintain in the midst. I want you to take today and handle one situation or person differently. If you don't say, "Good Morning," today speak and say, "Good Morning." If you're fussing about that bill, begin to think positive and say, "It shall be paid." Once you speak it you will even feel better. Don't let that negativity overcome you—stay positive.

Proverbs 23:7

VALUE "KNOW YOUR WORTH"

Let's stop for a moment, I want you to ask yourself these questions:

Have you ever started seeing yourself through the eyes of those who don't value you?

Are you constantly trying to prove yourself to someone who has forgotten your value?

LAST BUT NOT LEAST...

Never let your self-worth depend on the acceptance of others.

Before creation God created you for Himself. He never intended for you to look for confidence in yourself, He said, "I'll be your confidence." He made us a chosen people and royal priesthood, a holy nation, a people for His own possession. Stop doubting yourself, God loves you and you are so valuable to Him.

1 Peter 2:9

EVERLASTING LOVE "YOUR FOREVER"

Just thinking of someone loving you forever, no matter what, is the best feeling in the world. I know I don't even have enough fingers to count how many people I thought were friends but left my life due to life's situations. I know that's happened to you, and sometimes it can be very painful. Then often I thought, *Well, if the pain didn't come, it wouldn't have pushed me to be there for the ones who have been there always.* God desires to be your forever, never leave you. We may feel like we have left Him, but He never leaves us. On this day, I pray you open your heart and embrace your forever. He loves you forever.

Psalms 86:15

REBORN "I AM"

On this day the last application of your total makeover. I want you to declare:

I am called by God 2Tim 1:9

I am being changed in His likeness 2 Corinthians 3:8

I am His temple 1 Corinthians 6:19

I am blessed Jeremiah 17:7

I am above and not beneath Deuteronomy 28:13

I am fearfully and wonderfully made Psalms 139:14

I am victorious Revelation 12:11

I will shine

I will produce

I accept myself

I accept my forever

JUST BELIEVE!

Genesis 15:2–6

God showed Abram a vision that he would have children as many as the stars in the sky. At that time Abram was in old age with no children. Abram believed God! He had faith in God's promise. To have faith in God is to trust Him. Hebrews 11:1 says, "Now faith is the substance of things hoped for, the evidence of things not seen." Has God ever shown you a vision? What was your response to the vision? Did you believe what God was showing you in the vision? In my walk with God, He showed me in a vision that He wanted me to open up a transitional home for young women presently in or have aged out of the foster care system. I laughed. "God, are you really serious?" I told God, "I'm not business minded, I'm shy, and I failed speech class twice in college. I can't speak, I have no resources. I have no money," and the list went on and on. In 2003, I picked up the vision and put it back down. I told God, "It's too hard and I can't do it!" Years went by and I got really frustrated and tired of my life situations.

I remember, one day, I sat on my bed and cried out to God saying, "There has to be more to life than this. God, please help me!" God spoke to my spirit and said, "Pick up the vision I showed you and trust me!"

I began meditating and believing God's Word. Philippians 4:13: "I can do all things through Christ which strengthened me..." Matthew 19:26: "With God all things are possible." As I began standing on God's Word my faith and confidence in Him increased! I began to say to myself, "I can really do what God says I can do!" Then weeks went by and I met someone who was very knowledgeable about youths who aged out of the foster system. Then the doors started to open when I moved by faith and believed God's Word.

As I continued to move in faith the doors began to open... Help came, resources came. I encourage you today that when God shows you a vision just believe Him! God promises that His vision that He showed you will come to pass if you Believe! God wants to bring us to be in a place of faith... Faith is active... It is not only good to believe, but you have to put action to it.

It's impossible to please God without faith. God moves by our faith; yes, it might look impossible in your eyes, but all things are possible with God. Some of you reading this journal, God showed you a vision that you will open up a business, publish a book, write songs, teach, preach, open up a shelter, write plays, produce music, write poetry and you ask God, "Can it really happen?"

God is saying, "Today, yes ... if you believe!"

I remember one day seeking the Lord and He laid on my heart to start working on getting the transitional home up and running. I said, "Okay God," even though the business account did not line up with what God said... As I stayed before the Lord, I received a phone call from an owner who builds homes and he stated that he would like to help the organization in any way he could. We met. In the meeting he said something very profound: "I can never out-give God." This company went on to build K.I.S.H. Home, Inc. from the ground up...

What God showed me is to believe even when it looks impossible in the natural. It is already done in the spiritual realm. Just Believe! Believe the vision God has shown you and it will come to pass, but you have to Believe! No matter what it looks like right now! Just Believe!

Thought for Today: When you have a dream, just believe that all things are possible with God!

WALKING IN GOD'S BEST

Scripture Reading: Luke 5:3-6, and 8

God wants you to walk in His Best! God loves you and has a purpose for your life! He doesn't want you to be like the man who lay in the bed for 38 years! This man lay in bed next to those who were blind, those who couldn't walk and those who could hardly move. God is saying, "Stop lying in the bed hanging around blind people. People with no Vision! People with no Faith! People with no Dreams! People who are negative and small-minded! Stop surrounding yourself with people who can't walk and those who can hardly move!"

These people are stuck in their thinking. They do not think outside of the box! These people put limits on God! God is trying to do a new thing and they are stuck in their thinking; telling you that you are too old to go back to school, you don't have the resources to open your business, you can't write the book or song, etc. God is saying, "Stop hanging around Dream Killers!"

TESTIMONY

I remember a time in my life when I hung around friends who were always negative. They thought nothing of me. I remember getting a job in my degree field. I was so excited because I was working in a restaurant with a psychology degree and I finally got a job in my field! I picked up the phone and called my friend. I told her about the promotion. The phone went silent... I want to encourage you that you have to be very careful who you tell your dreams to! On the other end of the phone, the person answered and said, "Who told you God wants you to leave the restaurant?" When I got off the phone, I was tired of all the negativity. I prayed to God for better friends. I have friends who will speak life into me and who are not competitive or jealous of where and what God is doing in my life to build the kingdom of God.

You have to surround yourself with positive people. People with Faith! People with Vision and Dreams; people who will inspire, empower and motive you and push you into your destiny! It's time to stop lying in the bed year after year after year! Stop lying in the bed like the man in verse 5 who was disabled for 38 years. If you have been saying to yourself, *I will open the business, write the stage play, and write songs, write a book, open a shelter, a daycare, preach, teach,* etc. year after year after year and never made a move, you just feel stuck! *Where do I start? Where will I get resources from?* God is saying to believe and stand on His Word! Decree and declare Mark 10:27, for with God all things are possible, and Psalm 23—The Lord is my shepherd, I shall not want.

If you believe God wants you to walk in His best ... birth out you dreams ... then take up your bed and walk! Walk By Faith and not by sight! Don't look to the right or to the left; keep your eyes on Jesus! He will guide you! He will give you all the directions you need! He will make your crooked way straight. God wants to do great things in your life! There is greatness inside of you! God will use you to do great exploits to build His kingdom! No matter what your life looks like right now, Walk By Faith and not By Sight.

---- God Wants to do a New Thing in Your Life!

----Walk into Your Calling!

----Walk into Your Dreams!

----Walk into Your Victory!

----Walk into Your Business!

----Walk into Your Ministry!

----Walk into Divine Connections!

----Walk into Your Destiny!

Pick up your Bed and Walk, Walk, Walk! Walk into God's Best!

Thought for today: I decree and declare that I will walk in God's Best! I am the head and not the tail! I will walk into my Dreams!

Awaken the Dreamer Journal

Write down all the dreams you would like to achieve this year.

_____

_____

_____

_____

_____

_____

_____

_____

_____

_____

_____

_____

_____

_____

_____

_____

_____

_____

What are the missions for your dreams?

_____

_____

_____

_____

_____

_____

_____

_____

_____

_____

_____

_____

_____

_____

_____

_____

_____

_____

_____

_____

_____

What are the visions for your DREAMS?

_____

_____

_____

_____

_____

_____

_____

_____

_____

_____

_____

_____

_____

_____

_____

_____

_____

_____

_____

_____

_____

_____

What is your passion?

_____

_____

_____

_____

_____

_____

_____

_____

_____

_____

_____

_____

_____

_____

_____

_____

_____

_____

_____

_____

What are the steps you will take to pursue your dreams?

_____

_____

_____

_____

_____

_____

_____

_____

_____

_____

_____

_____

_____

_____

_____

_____

_____

_____

_____

_____

_____

Create a vision board of pictures of your dreams this year. • Write down what pictures you will use for your vision board as a guide*

_____

_____

_____

_____

_____

_____

_____

_____

_____

_____

_____

_____

_____

_____

_____

_____

_____

_____

_____

_____

_____

_____

Write down the scriptures you will meditate on while pursing your DREAMS.

_____

_____

_____

_____

_____

_____

_____

_____

_____

_____

_____

_____

_____

_____

_____

_____

_____

_____

_____

_____

_____

the timeframe in which you would like to achieve your dreams;
one month, six months, 12 months or longer.

• ONE MONTH

_____

_____

_____

_____

_____

_____

_____

_____

_____

_____

_____

_____

_____

_____

_____

_____

_____

_____

• SIX MONTHS

• TWELVE MONTHS

Author Bios & Acknowledgments

Quonda J Warner

Was born and raised in Philadelphia, PA. At the age of eleven she accepted God into her life at the Bible Way Baptist Church under the leadership of Dr. Damone B. And Dr. Melissa Jones in West Philadelphia. From that moment on she has kept the faith through the good and rough times in her life. Just to name a few, Quonda is a graduate of Archbishop Prendergast high school, Everest University, Melvin Floyd school of evangelism, Touched by the Hands of Grace academy, and Trish M School of the Prophetic and Mercer County Community College. Quonda always knew there was a call on her life, but early in her life she just could not figure it out until she developed a closer relationship with God. From her relationship with Christ she has become a wife, mother, intercessor, entrepreneur, CEO /founder of Expressions of Kindness cleaning service and much more. The Church of your Destiny in Williamstown, NJ under the leadership of Bishop Edward and Lady Ann Wilson is where Quonda currently fellowships along with her loving husband Lewis and two children, Jair and Sophia.

QUONDA'S ACKNOWLEDGEMENTS.......

I would like to thank my Lord and Savior Jesus Christ for keeping, loving and grooming me for such a time as this! To my father Ivan who was a great disciplinarian. I may have not enjoyed it growing up, but I truly appreciate it now and all the sacrifices you've made by putting me in the best schools! To my mom Marie, for allowing me to be birthed and raised up in the way I should go. You were and still are always there for me. From phone calls to giving of gifts and outings I will never forget them. My siblings Nadia, Mark, Brittany and Ani I love you all for our many laughs and memories. You were my first true friends! To Julia Pierre, you have walked with me through my toughest times in life and made sure that I got to live out one of my dreams, which was to be married! Dr. Kishma for pushing me further in my purpose and challenging me to give it my all! Last but not least, to my best friend, God-fearing, handsome husband Lou for always supporting, providing and loving me unconditionally. You prayed for me and my vision, laid hands on me when I was sick and I was healed! I could write a whole book about you! To the many others, I love you all!

Sandra Jackson

Has been listed in *Kish Magazine*; she will be honored in July 2020 for Women of Strength; she has appeared on the *Lady Flava Show*. Sandra has facilitated numerous support groups in her community. She has a couple support groups, one of which is called Breathe Again, a support group for caregivers of children with special needs and their families. Sandra was ordained in 2008 as an Ordained Minister. Empowered Women of God Ministry was birthed from that point. Empowered Women of God Ministry's mission is to empower, inspire and assist all women from all walks of life to be the best they can be with applying the Word of God to their lives. Sandra's prayer is that all humans give their lives to Jesus and live how the Word of God says we should live.

Sandra now is opening a place called The Inpowerment Room, she knows that healing starts from within, a place of inspiration and growth.

Sandra continues to allow the love of God to shine through her. She continues to do the will of God as He leads her.

SANDRA'S ACKNOWLEDGEMENTS...

I want to give God all the praise and honor, I thank Him for bringing me on this journey. I thank you for all that you do from waking me up to allowing me to breathe. I thank you for what you have placed in me; I thank you for the connections and relationships that you have brought into my life. You are so amazing you blow my mind often, thank you.

I want to thank my mother Elaine Jackson, my queen and best friend, I love you so much. Thanks for always being there and giving me unconditional love, for showing me what strength looks like; you are an amazing woman, I am so blessed to have you as my mother, I love and respect you as my queen.

I want to thank my dad; he was Harold Young (RIP) who taught me so much in life. He taught how it is to be the apple of a man's eye; he loved me so much; he taught me the good, bad and the ugly of how this world can be. I will always be your HAM; love you forever and always.

I want to thank my children Naeem, Kareem, Shunnar, Isaiah, Jovan and my goddaughter Jasmine for being some of my greatest teachers, they have taught me how self-less, forgiving, loving and strong I am because I love them and want the best for them. I push so hard because I want you to know you can do what you put your mind to; no matter how many obstacles come your way, you are overcomers. You all are extraordinary; I hope my life has displayed that you don't have to be a follower to be a Trailblazer. I love you all.

I want to thank my grandchildren Gracie, Leilanie, Ava, Zynae', Antoine and Antonio for always bringing sunshine into my life, I love you all. I hope you all carry on my legacy.

I want to thank all my siblings Annette, Marie, Jeanette, Ebony, Charles and Leon for loving me unconditionally. I love you all.

I have an amazing bunch of nieces, great nieces, nephews, and great nephews. To my amazing aunts, uncles, cousins, friends and acquaintances, I love you.

I want to thank my mentor Kishma George for taking the time to invest in me some of her jewels so unselfishly; we need more midwives in the Kingdom to help us push our dreams to a reality. I thank you Kishma for giving me a chance to display some of my jewels, I pray that she prospers in all she does. Thank you for pushing me.

I want to thank Mrs. Sargis (RIP), she was the best teacher; she always told me failure was not an option. She pushed me from grade 8, she said I would not be ordinary I would be extraordinary. I thank God for her impact on my life.

To all the caregivers that have children with special needs, I tip my hat to you. Keep doing what you are doing and continue to look to the hills from whence cometh your help. I love you, you are not alone. You are amazing vessels that God uses for our children—thank you.

Renee Denise Laws

Elder Renee Denise Laws is a native of Baltimore, Maryland and the founder of Helping Others Win (H.O.W.) Ministry.

The purpose for the inception of H.O.W. is to equip God's people to win physically and spiritually in love through life applications, biblical teachings and the Spoken Word. The H.O.W. Ministry offers a holistic approach to help heal the mind, body, soul and spirit of God's people.

In 1997, Elder Renee answered the first call to salvation at Imani Christian Fellowship Church.

In 1999, she answered the call to Ministry. In 2000, she received her biblical education under Kingdom Worship Center.

In 2007, Elder Renee was ordained under the Leadership on Kingdom Center Ministries, Inc. where her gifts of intercession and of Helps flourished.

In 2008, with the guidance of the Holy Spirit she began mentoring women around the world; helping them to excel to a greater level in God. In addition, she helps them to maximize their potential, know their self-worth, use their gifts and abilities to fulfill purpose, and teach them how to be strategic in every area of their lives.

In 2015, Elder Renee opened her first transitional house in West Baltimore for women and children and in 2016, she opened her second transitional house in Northeast Baltimore.

In 2019, she received her certification in bereavement support from Roberta's House.

Elder Renee walks in the wisdom and favor of God. She has the ability to operate in several capacities, which are great assets to the Kingdom of God. She is extremely passionate about promoting positive thinking and excellence into the lives of women.

Elder Renee firmly believes that spiritual and natural growth are vital ingredients needed to aspire women to pursue and conquer their dreams and to stand the tests of time in order to make a difference in their lives.

Her commitment to excellence has been recognized by many women around the world. Since she takes pleasure in the family structure, spending time with her daughters, Natasha and Nicole, is an important part of her life. Her favorite scripture is Jeremiah 29:11, which states, "For I know the plans I have for you, declares the Lord; plans to prosper you and not to harm you, plans to give you hope and a future."

She is currently serving at New Covenant Life Ministry under the covering of Bishop Randolph Adams and Overseer Tanya M. Adams.

PRAYER OF THANKS...

FATHER God, thank you for abiding in me apart from you I can't do anything but with you all things are possible. So, I put my dreams, hopes and desires in your hands. I trust you with my life. Thank you for giving me your wisdom, knowledge and understanding to complete whatever it takes to make my dream rise. In Jesus' name, Amen.

Father God, thank you forgiving me before I move forward in the steps you have ordered for my life. I want to thank you for the power to forgive those who have hurt me and the strength to release any resentment and bitterness that I am still holding on to that could have an impact on the manifestation of my dream coming true . In Jesus' name, Amen.

FATHER God, thank you for your perfect timing. Sometimes, it just doesn't make sense how things will even work together for my good. Teach me while I wait patiently in you to enjoy each and every moment of my dream journey, knowing that You who started a good work in me will complete it. In Jesus' name, Amen.

RENEE'S ACKNOWLEDGEMENTS ...

To my Heavenly Father, I acknowledge you first and foremost. Thank you for giving me life and making my dreams a reality. Thank you for walking with me through it all. I thank you for sacrificing your son Jesus Christ who covers and intercedes for me daily. I thank you for your Holy Spirit who comforts and guides me that I will never be deceived. Heavenly Father, I dedicate this book to you. All the glory, honor and praises belong to you.

To my mom and dad, thank you for being wonderful examples. Thank you for loving me and bestowing family values and principles. Thank you for imparting wisdom and your extraordinary generosity. I am forever grateful.

To my twin girls who I love to life, thank you for being my cheerleaders and my greatest supporters. Thank you for your love and patience. Your sacrifice has been duly noted for all you have done for me. It has been my pleasure to raise two phenomenal daughters. I am honored to be your mother.

To my brother and sister, thank you for your unending support and love. Thank you for allowing me to be me. Thank you for always speaking truth. I am blessed.

To my mentees, thank you for making me the best possible mentor I can be. Thank you for stretching me and challenging me to be all I can be for God. Thank you for your continuous love, prayers and motivation. I am truly appreciative.

To my family and friends, thank you for believing in me and encouraging me that I can do all things through Christ who strengthens me. Thank you standing with me; by faith I am victorious.

To my spiritual parents, thank you for all your selfless love from infancy. Thank you for raising me to have strong faith, pray continually and give God my very best. Thank you for teaching me to first be a servant and second to equip God's people for works of service. I am forever favored.

To my pastors, thank you for your constant encouragement and consistent prayers. Thank you for investing your time and talents. Thank you for your love that lifted me in the most difficult times of my life. I am tremendously blessed.

Special thanks to you for giving me the opportunity and a chance to fulfill my dreams. Thank you for allowing me to share with you what God gave me for you. Thanks to everyone who participated in bringing this book to life. God is truly a Promise Keeper.

LET'S STAY CONNECTED

Email address: reneedlaws@gmail.com

Website: www.reneedlaws.com

Facebook: Renee D Laws

Instagram address: how_ministries

Instagram address: how_ministries

I would love to hear from you about how you were encouraged, made healthy or blessed by this book.

I speak to the Dreamer in you.

Feel free to inquire about my availability for speaking engagements at churches or organizations or events.

Thank you!

Shawnette Braxton

Shawnette Braxton can in a single word be described as an encourager.

She is an entrepreneur, coach, mentor, trailblazer, and altruist.

Shawnette is a passionate speaker and mentor and it is fulfilled through the Dreams Come True mentoring program in Baltimore Maryland. She believes despite life's tests and trials, you were created on purpose for a purpose. Shawnette is the CEO of JALU Collection Clothing Company (Jesus Always Loves U), which was founded out of a dark and painful season in her life. Shawnette has one son. She is a graduate of Carver Vocational Technical High School class of 2000.

VISION

Shawnette Braxton of JALU Collection leads in creating fashionable clothing for men and women, and she will soon release a clothing brand for kids.

She informs, educates, consults and maintains great customer service for her products, an integral part of an accessible, quality-based clothing brand.

SHAWNETTE'S ACKNOWLEDGEMENTS...

A special thank you to my Lord and Savior Jesus Christ who allowed this moment to happen for me. I would like to thank my lovely son, my little mini me, for his prayers and his encouragement, my spiritual mentor who was such a big encouragement through this whole process with pushing me through, also my business mentor who was such an inspiration to me on the business aspect of my life and helped me to use faith and not fear concerning my business endeavors.

To my parents and sister and my immediate family I just want to say thank you for all your prayers and encouraging words that never go unnoticed. God bless you and continue to keep you in perfect peace. I would love to thank Bishop Randolph and Overseer Tanya M Adams and the New Covenant Life Ministry for all your support and prayers. Thank you.

CONTACT INFORMATION...

Shawnette Braxton
CEO/Founder
Jalu Collection
Shawnettenbraxton@gmail.com
www.shawnettebraxton.com
www.Jalucollection.com
Facebook:Shawnette Braxton

Periscope@ShawnetteBraxton
Personal Number: (240)319-6211
Office: (667)207-1247

Pristina Melton

Pristina is an Esthetician, Massage Therapist, a Nursing Assistant and a former graduate of Cosmetology School. She was born in Dover, DE, where she spent most of her life. She is a sister of six sisters and three brothers, and a mother of two children Paris Melton and Prince Melton. Despite her own difficulties in life, she has always tried to find beauty and positivity in everything. She always says, "There's nothing too hard for God." Every day she thanks God for the ability to help heal and flourish the body both internally and externally. Whether it be leaving spiritual nuggets for her clients battling depression or sickness, relieving their pain and tension or and hearing their release as they take that deep breath, she always finds a blessing. I hope that as you read this book it inspires you, and you feel so refreshed, glowing in confidence that you are Royalty.

Email: Urhighness7107@gmail.com

Phone Number: 302-538-4079

Business to Come: Urhighness Total Makeover

PRISTINA'S ACKNOWLEDGEMENTS

This book was based on my walk with Christ and others. Often in my career path, as a Massage Therapist, Esthetician, and a past Cosmetologist, I always sought to make people feel and look beautiful. Even though we can make them look amazing on the outside, there was something they needed to grasp internally. I want to acknowledge God first and my walk with Him. The amazing Kishma George, who put this book project together, believed in and me helped me accomplish this goal. To my kids' godparent, Ms. Angela Cosey, my godmother Mrs. Ojetta Chaplin and my clients, thanks for listening to me over and over again as I tried to strategize what to say. Last but not least, thank you to my kids Paris Melton & Prince Melton, and my niece Diamond Lovett who mean so much to me and have taught me some of the most valuable lessons as being their mother and auntie. I love them until infinity. They all kept me going, this project would have been impossible without them.

Dr. Kishma A. George

Dr. Kishma A. George can, in a single phrase, be described as a Purpose Pusher. She is a prophetess, entrepreneur, inspirational speaker, international radio personality, TV show host and guest, mentor, playwright, producer and 4x best-selling author, and her overarching mission is to inspire people to fulfill their God-given purpose. She believes that despite life's circumstances, there is greatness inside of you! Dr. Kishma's work as a speaker and mentor is executed through the Women Destined for Greatness Mentoring Program in Kent County, Delaware.

Dr. Kishma A. George is the preisdent and CEO of K.I.S.H. (Kingdom Investments in Single Hearts) Home, Inc. K.I.S.H. Home, Inc. was founded out of the desire to make an impact in the lives of girls and women in Delaware, as well as those young women who are presently in or have aged out of the foster care system. As an independent living mentor Kishma witnessed the tremendous challenges that aged-out foster care youth experienced while trying to find their way to a self-sufficient and stable life.

A passion within her grew for these young adults and their future as she experienced their frustration in handling basic skills, such as opening a checking/savings account, parenting and the frustration of single parenthood. Ms. George knew that these young adults, whether they were a single parent or single, needed a strong support system that would empower and encourage them to take control of their lives. They struggled in their transition of leaving their homes or foster care because many were still attending high school and were not emotionally or financially stable.

After witnessing this, Ms. George began her journey of seeking ways to assist young adults in becoming emotionally and economically self-sufficient so that their transition out of their homes or the foster care system and into independent living was successful. Many of the young adults with whom she worked left their homes or foster care at 18 years old and found themselves homeless, pregnant, lacking self-esteem, incarcerated, unemployed and without guidance. As a mentor, Ms. George became frustrated by the minimum amount of resources the community offered these young adults. She wanted to make a difference in their lives and make certain that they had a safe, successful transition to adulthood and independent living.

K.I.S.H. Home, Inc. offers young women in Delaware the support they need to become emotionally stable and self-sufficient in every aspect of their lives and community.

Her diligence and passion for young women have been recognized in various newspaper articles, including in the *Dover Post*, *Delaware News Journal*, *Delaware State News*, and *Milford Beacon*. She was also featured in the *Kingdom Voices Magazine, Gospel 4 U Magazine, K.I.S.H. Magazine*, BOND Inc., and BlogSpot's week spotlight "Fostered Out of Love". In addition to appearing as special guest on the *Atlanta LIVE* TV show, *Life Talk* radio show with Coach TMB, live TV show *Straight Talk for Women Only*, and The *Frank and Travis* radio show on Praise 105.1.

Empowered Women Ministries have recognized Dr. Kishma as Woman of the Year in the category of Entrepreneurial Success, as well as Zeta Phi Beta Sorority, Inc. / Theta Zeta Zeta Chapter for her outstanding involvement in the Greater Dover Community. She was also presented with the Diversity Award (2013) from the State of Delaware / Social Services, the Authentic Servant Leadership Award (2014) & New Castle County Chapter of the DSU Alumni Association 33rd annual scholarship luncheon for outstanding service to the Wilmington Community and the Delaware State University (2014), Church Girlz Rock (2015); Humanitarian Award (2015), Faith Fighter Award (2016), Business Woman of the Year (2106), CHOICES "Woman of the Year" (2016) and Global Smashers Award (2017). Business Woman of the Year Award (2018), I AM Baby Doll Global Award (2018), I AM Entrepreneurship Devorah Award (2018), I AM Fabulous Award (2019), Phenomenal Woman of the Year (2019), World-Changer Award (2019). Dr. Kishma received her Bachelor of Science degree in Psychology from Delaware State University & an Honorary Doctor of Philosophy; Humane Letters from CICA

International University & Seminary. Her passion is to empower you through the Word of God and inspire you to begin living your DREAMS. No matter what your circumstances may be, God has a purpose for your life.

Dr. Kishma strives to make a difference in your life and make certain that YOU will birth EVERY DREAM God has placed on the inside. Dr. Kishma A. George is the director of the Women Destined for Greatness Mentoring Program and visionary/editor-in-chief for *K.I.S.H. Magazine*. To Contact Kishma A. George visit www.kishmageorge.com

DR. KISHMA'S ACKNOWLEDGEMENTS

First and foremost, I want to give God all the glory and honor, as He made this vision possible. I love you, Lord, with all my heart! ♡ In memory of my beloved father, Edmond Felix George; I am thankful for his encouragement and inspiring me to dream. ♡ To the best mother in the world, Novita Scatliffe-George; I thank you for your love, support, encouraging words and praying for me. Thank you for not giving up on me. I love you, Mom! ♡ To my wonderful daughter Kiniquá, I love you dearly. Thank you for your encouraging words, hugs and love. ♡ To my family, James, Raeisha, Christopher, Joshua, Seriah, Janisha and Kayla— thank you for supporting the vision with your prayers and love. ♡ Thank you Toy James and Abena Mc Clean for your prayers, support and encouraging me to pursue my dreams. I thank God that you are my special friends. Love you, ladies ♡

A special thank you to the co-authors of *Awaken the Dreamer*; Pristina Melton, Shawnette Braxton, Quonda Warner,

Renee Laws and Sandra Jackson

A special thank you my beautiful Jackie Hicks for her amazing photography, beautiful Letitia Thornhill for her gift of makeup artistry, beautiful Sonja Alston for an amazing hairstyle! Love you, ladies! ♡ To K.I.S.H. Home, Inc.'s board/advisors, volunteers and mentors; thank you for your dedication, support and believing in the vision of helping make a difference in the lives of young women in Delaware. To Emily Ann Warren, thank you for your support, love, and believing in me. To Pastor Ayanna, Publisher; I thank God, every day for bringing you into my life. You have been a blessing. Thank you for your encouraging words, support, love and believing in the vision.

Love you♡ Lastly, but not least, I would like to thank CTS graphics, ChosenButterfly Publishing and everyone who encouraged, prayed for and supported K.I.S.H. Home, Inc. over the years, I am forever grateful. God Bless!

Made in the USA
Middletown, DE
17 April 2021